Operation New Freedom

12 STEPS
EMBRACED
WITH A MILITARY
MINDSET

Operation New Freedom

12 STEPS
EMBRACED
WITH A MILITARY
MINDSET

JONATHAN D.

CONTENTS

Acknowledgments vii

Introduction ix

Answering The Call xvii

Step 1:   Move To The Winning Side 1

Step 2:   The Calvary Has Arrived 9

Step 3:   The Situation Is Well In Hand 19

Step 4:	Gathering Intelligence	29
Step 5:	Band Of Brothers And Sisters	39
Step 6:	The Next Evolution	47
Step 7:	Weakness Leaving The Body	53
Step 8:	Damage Control	59
Step 9:	Responsibility For Our Actions	67
Step 10:	Assessment Of The Situation	75
Step 11:	Marching Orders	83
Step 12:	No One Left Behind	91

The Twelve Steps Of Alcoholics Anonymous*.. 99

ACKNOWLEDGMENTS

I would like to give thanks to Lynn Bright, Frank Canfield, Mike Matthews, Tom Wright, Phil Bernstein, and Matt Brady for all their help, support, and feedback during the writing process. Thank you to God as I understand him for a new life and all the men and women of the Armed Forces who serve or have served this great nation of ours. Finally, a special thanks to Bill W. and Dr. Bob, and everyone who is and has been a part of my recovery. I love you more than words can express.

Copyright All Rights Reserved ©

INTRODUCTION

I began drinking in the United States Marine Corps. It's no secret Marines like to drink. Consuming alcohol and raising Hell are accepted and expected forms of recreation. I don't blame the Marine Corps one bit for me being an alcoholic. There are many Marines who serve our country every day who don't touch one drop of alcohol.

Within a few a few short years after enlisting, I was a full-blown alcoholic. I did manage to get an honorable discharge, even though my drinking affected my performance as well as my mental and physical health. I brought the disease back home and continued to sink further and further into the pit of alcoholism. It took a second drunk-driving conviction to finally get me into the fellowship of Alcoholics Anonymous. I had no interest in attending meetings, but a condition of my probation mandated ten meetings. A violation could have resulted in jail time.

I was quite skeptical and had many misconceptions about Alcoholics Anonymous. However, I kept an open mind and listened to what everyone had to say. My life has never been the same since. I found the structure, discipline and camaraderie I had been missing since my days in the service.

At first, I thought the steps were incompatible with my military training. Admit I'm powerless and that my life is unmanageable? It would be a cold day in Hell before I admitted defeat. Turn my life and will over to a perceived dictatorial higher power? Not a chance. My misunderstandings changed the more I studied the steps and went to meetings. I soon discovered common threads between my military background and the twelve step program and fellowship.

The transformation that takes place in the military and AA meetings is phenomenal. In the former, recruits from all walks of life are molded and shaped to become part of the mightiest military force the world has ever known. Men and women are essentially "broken down" and then are rebuilt to become an integral part of a highly specialized team. Likewise, twelve step meetings also change its members into something extraordinary. The change can last for a lifetime and often does.

I'm an alcoholic, and I will be sharing my thoughts on recovery mostly from that perspective, but it must be emphasized that the twelve steps have been used successfully to treat a whole host of addictions and compulsions. I certainly sympathize with individuals addicted to narcotics and opiates, but I must confess that I believe they don't speak my language on some levels.

The disease of addiction can manifest in many different forms. Ultimately, it doesn't matter what our individual drug of choice is because our thinking is the real problem. I have a mind that isn't always my best friend. The only hope for me is that a power greater than myself produces the much needed change in my consciousness that will lead me to recovery.

I don't push my conception of a higher power on anyone because I know how long it took me to reestablish my spiritual connection. Veterans and service members come into the fellowship with a variety of faiths or none at all. I've personally witnessed people stay sober who subscribe to many different conceptions of a power greater than themselves. My faith in the Lord keeps me sober today, and I will share that faith with anyone who's interested. I just don't find it necessary to force my beliefs on anyone who attends a meeting for the first time.

I salute veterans and service members of every branch of our Armed Forces. I look to them for leadership and inspiration. America's finest sons and daughters constitute the best military the world has ever seen. Members from every branch have taught me valuable lessons about life and recovery. I am a United States Marine and can only share from that perspective. It is not my intention for any branch of service to feel slighted or neglected in any way.

It is my hope that this little book can enhance the recovery of any veteran, active or otherwise, who struggles with addiction. I want nothing more than to see the outstanding individuals of our military achieve final victory and enjoy a clean, happy, and successful life for many years to come. It is also my hope that anyone can use this book to embrace their recovery with a military mindset. There is a tremendous amount of freedom that can be experienced when one decides to implement the twelve steps into their life. I decided to call this little book "Operation New Freedom", because I want everyone to experience liberation in every sense of the word. Only then can life truly be enjoyed.

Answering the call

America's finest sons and daughters have always stepped up and answered their country's call in times of emergency and crises throughout the years. They have sacrificed everything to serve a cause greater than themselves. Their selfless acts of dedication and sense of duty are without equal.

The scourge of addiction is a threat that must be answered with a swift response. Veterans who have recovered from their addictions can now redirect their energy and efforts into a new campaign that's just as serious and deadly as those in the past. The time for action has never been more urgent.

Veterans can provide a mindset and perspective to battling addiction that's truly unique. We excel in thinking creatively and unconventionally. Such an approach is critical in countering an enemy that doesn't subscribe to concepts like decency and morality. I urge all my fellow veterans to answer the call and help win the battle against addiction. Our families, communities, and country have never needed us as much as they do now.

STEP ONE

MOVE TO THE WINNING SIDE

*We admitted we were powerless over alcohol-that
our lives had become unmanageable.*

The word "surrender" is not a part of the vocabulary of most veterans. Surrendering contradicts everything that we were taught in training. The American society in general looks down on the idea of giving up. Americans love to win and achieve; second place just doesn't

Jonathan D.

cut it. In fact, second place is considered the first loser. All the runner-up gets is a nice set of steak knives.

Everyone wants to be the best. Rarely do you hear young people say they want to grow up and become the Vice President of our country or a Fortune 500 company. The military culture takes winning to an even higher level. The American society absolutely demands military victory in every single engagement it's involved in.

I remember my company commander from job training telling us that our job as marines was to kill America's enemies when we were called upon to do so. He strongly emphasized that there should be no doubt in our minds regarding our main purpose. I remember the constant reminders of how good the United States Marine Corps was as a first-class organization during the early days of boot camp. We were repeatedly told that we were the best and had no equals. Only U.S. Marines are qualified to guard the President of The United States. The Marine Corps is an organization of killing machines that will swiftly defeat anyone who chooses to take them on.

Now, picture having this mindset and walking into a meeting of Alcoholics Anonymous and essentially being informed in step one that the only way you're going to recover and get better is to admit complete defeat. One can imagine the difficulty some veterans and Marines have with this concept of giving up in order to win. The idea of surrendering goes against everything veterans represent and fight for. Some will go to their graves still seeking an excuse to win the fight and drink like a "normal" person. Improvising, adapting, and overcoming a challenge is a more appealing option than throwing in the towel to us veterans.

A never-say-die approach can be successful in life and war. There have been countless battles won by sheer grit and persistence. Sooner or later, an individual or an army will break if enough pressure is applied on them.

The problem is that alcoholism is a disease that's extremely cunning, mysterious, and powerful. The words crafty and immoral can also be added to the list. The war with alcohol is one where the rules of engagement don't apply. The disease of addiction doesn't fight fair and will use every trick imaginable to destroy its unfortunate victim. The affliction can wait years if necessary for you to let your guard down for even a second. Then it will strike without warning, taking away everything you have achieved and worked for. Furthermore, the lives of family members and close friends may be in shambles as they watch you falling to pieces in horror.

Alcoholism and addiction in general are adversaries that allow little probability of defeating them in a head-to-head competition. So what's the solution? The military genius Sun Szu himself advised against getting into battles

Jonathan D.

that you have no chance of winning. The answer is to not get in the fight in the first place.

I can recall old-timers (members with 20 or more years in recovery) say at meetings that they never want to get back into the ring with that six hundred pound gorilla called alcoholism. As strange as it sounds, I have a better chance of victory if I choose not to fight. I win by surrendering.

I'll admit that it took me a long time to wrap my head around such a counter-intuitive concept. It went against everything I believed in and was taught since childhood. But the simple truth remains that I can't get drunk if I don't pick up a drink; I won't get beaten to a pulp if I don't participate in the fight.

Alcoholism and addiction are enemies that don't play fair or nice. Only a solution that seems implausible has a chance of solving a problem that defies all reason, logic, and common sense. The surrender-to-win method is the answer that solves the puzzle of addiction.

We are no less of men, women, veterans, or service members just because we became addicts. Admitting to being powerless takes a tremendous amount of courage. All the honor, integrity, and values instilled during basic military training are not compromised in any way by admitting defeat.

I once over-heard a Marine share his perspective on the first step and it has stayed with me throughout the years. He said to think of step one in terms of "moving to the winning side". Why not move to the side that produces success and a happy life? Why stay on the side that constantly leads to failure, misery, and defeat?

I quite like being part of the solution instead of the problem. What started me on the winning path was to admit that alcohol had me down for the count. My life only started to get better once I admitted defeat. It feels so good to be on the winning side today.

Step one is just the beginning. Veterans and service members suffering from addiction can reclaim that awesome feeling that comes from victory. The path to get there is unusual for sure, but we as addicts are in a war that must be won at any and all costs.

STEP TWO
THE CALVARY HAS ARRIVED

Came to believe that a Power greater than ourselves could restore us to sanity.

Step two is the step of hope; it's the step when the calvary arrives in full force and begins to turn the tide of the war on addiction. There is finally light at the end of the tunnel after years and years of catastrophic defeats and setbacks. A power greater than me came into my life and brought about the necessary psychological change required for me to recover from the hopeless condition of alcoholism. The Navy Seals have a saying I'm extremely fond of. Seals are "never out of the fight". There's always hope and a chance to snatch victory from the jaws of defeat. I don't care how many times a person has been knocked down by the disease of addiction. A power greater than ourselves is the game changer that never fails. Step two is special to me because I actually experienced step two before step one. I had to be restored to sanity long enough to surrender in order to be restored to sanity again.

I had to call my employer to bail me out of jail after I had been arrested for drunk driving for a second time. It was degrading and humiliating to be caught in a company van and have it impounded. However, my employer showed signs that a power greater than me was working through him on my behalf because he graciously posted bail and I was released from the county jail.

The madness and insanity of alcoholism in my life didn't end there. I retrieved the van from the impound lot and went back to my motel room. The small refrigerator had a couple of cans of beer left in it from the previous night. I grabbed a can and started drinking again only hours after being bailed out of jail.

A power greater than myself must have decided I was beyond human aid. Alcohol was winning the war until reinforcements arrived on the scene. I started to drink a second beer and then stopped abruptly and poured the remainder down the sink. I haven't had a drink since. A psychological change took place in my consciousness, and the terrible grip alcohol had over me was broken.

My life was an absolute train wreck. I was on the verge of total destruction. One more strike would have put me out of the game for good. Everything in my life seemed hopeless. My physical, mental, and spiritual health was poor. I had very few friends, and I felt disconnected from God and society, but then a power greater than myself came into my life out of nowhere with the force of ten armies. The insanity of alcoholism finally met its match. Overwhelming power forced alcohol into submission. The power stormed into my mind the same way the Marines stormed the beaches at Normandy. I struck gold in my darkest hour and order was restored.

There was an old Sailor who had a profound impact on my life and recovery. He was a veteran who served in the United States Navy during World War Two. I was blessed to sit with him at numerous meetings. Step two was one of his favorites because his experience was similar to mine and had served him well because he had close to sixty years of uninterrupted sobriety before he passed away. I'll never forget his perspective on and experience with the second step.

Jonathan D.

My dear friend described in great detail how he had this merciless obsession with drinking alcohol for years on end. The obsession ravaged his life. He suffered humiliation and embarrassing moments. But One day, the obsession to drink disappeared. "Where did it go?" he would often ask. Why was it that one day he had an insane urge to keep drinking and the next day he didn't? The only explanation he found convincing was that a power greater than him had removed the obsession. The power came into that drunken Sailor's life and did for him what he had zero chance of doing himself.

A similar power restored me to sanity in a similar way. The obsession to consume alcohol dominated every aspect of my life. I was often intoxicated at the most inappropriate times. I would behave in a hateful manner and say hurtful things to my friends and family. One day, my foul infatuation with alcohol was removed from my consciousness; a power greater and stronger brought about a psychic change.

I felt like a prisoner of war who was freed in a rescue operation. Alcohol definitely had my mind twisted. I couldn't tell the true from the false and believed right was wrong and wrong was right. It was if alcohol had conducted a major brainwashing experiment in my head and turned me against myself and society. A power greater than me had to cleanse my mind with its magnificent influence and lead me back to the truth. I had to have years of damage undone so I could get squared away and be back on top.

It's important to point out that we addicts don't have to know exactly how this power works. The absence of a thorough explanation can prove problematic for veterans like me. We have been trained to pay close attention to every detail. I simply don't know how this power performed this miracle in my life with its "secret weapon". I don't have a scientific explanation for the intrinsic details of my psychic change.

I can say for certain that this power thrust itself into my mind with intensity and ferocity. Like the Marines and the Air Force, the power struck fast and hard, and the disease of alcoholism didn't know what hit it. A magnificent power landed in my mind and gave me hope for the first time in years. I'm profoundly grateful for being restored to sanity and being able to see the world in an entirely new perspective.

STEP THREE
THE SITUATION IS WELL IN HAND

Made a decision to turn our will and our lives over to the care of God <u>as we understood Him</u>.

Addiction doesn't subscribe to the rules of war. It will use every deceptive and unconventional tactic possible. Our disease wants us dead by any means necessary. However, we have an option that will allow us to create and set conditions that will work in our favor; we can

Jonathan D.

make a decision to turn our will and our lives over to the care of God as we understand him. As a result, the rules will be completely changed in a manner which will benefit us.

The disease of addiction is armed with nasty tricks and cheap shots. God as we understand him is our secret weapon. We have the opportunity to turn our lives over to a power that outmatches addiction and can't be beaten. God as we understand him is the game-changer that makes us unstoppable.

The state of our condition will be well in control. God as we understand him has declared martial law in our lives by restoring serenity, sanity, and order, and destructive and lawless behavior will no longer be tolerated. Addiction rendered my life chaotic and dysfunctional. My life was like a poorly functioning unit in dire need of a field commander. I choose to let God as I understand him be my permanent commander.

The power and leadership of God forced out the cruel and tyrannical control of addiction that kept me in a constant state of pain and terror. The addiction to alcohol no longer has free reign in my life; the disease has been overthrown. God as I understand him is in charge now.

There are still pockets of resistance that attack and harass the new regime God has established. But God's power cuts them down to size without mercy. The disease of addiction is shown that

Jonathan D.

it's no longer running the show. Refusal to accept that fact is futile.

I feel tremendously secure when God as I understand him is in control of my life. God is watching my back at all times. His power surrounds my entire existence. I think of God as a spiritual sniper sitting on top of heavenly buildings and clouds, just waiting to shoot anything or anyone who attempts to cause me harm.

God's protection instills confidence in us because we can live free of fear. We can pursue all our dreams and goals and accomplish our mission and objectives. The fear of failure doesn't even enter our minds, and we can be certain of succeeding because as long as God is with us, even ten armies couldn't prevail against us.

Just because God is with us doesn't mean we won't experience difficult times. Life is not fair and can be very unkind. Situations will arise that threaten our sobriety and serenity. Dear friends and loved ones will pass away. Supervisors and co-workers at our jobs will at times try to sabotage us every chance they get. Friends we have had for a long time will develop new patterns of behavior that make us uncomfortable. In fact, it will seem at times like the entire world is against us and the situation is hopeless.

That's when we will turn to God as we understand him. We will turn our lives over to a power that

Jonathan D.

can defeat any enemy or challenge we face. We get down on our knees and ask God to help us because he's the only one we can truly count on when the bullets start flying, and chaos begins to unfold.

Only God as we understand him can restore order to our lives, only God as we understand him can be the shield that blocks the bullets coming at us from every direction. In step three, we make the decision to turn our will and our <u>lives</u> over to the care of God as we understand him. We need to remember that God doesn't just protect us from the disease of addiction. He wants to protect us from every challenge and threat; God as we understand him wants to be in charge of every area of our lives.

The third step had to be chopped up into tiny pieces for me. It was a tough pill to swallow. I couldn't digest the thought of turning anything over to the care of God. I thought I would turn into nothing more than a slave who had no sense of autonomy, personality, or individuality.

I felt especially disgusted by the idea of kneeling before God. I was certain that God had abandoned me in my youth. I grew up in an environment that was sick, toxic, and depressing. Where was God during this time? My problem and anger with God began to dissipate when someone suggested I "act as if" God existed. The third step allowed me to have a conception of God that wasn't punishing or vengeful. I found a God of my own understanding who

Jonathan D.

was caring and forgiving. He didn't throw in my face the fact that I had to come crawling back to him and welcomed me with open arms.

After some time of "faking it until I made it", I actually started believing and acknowledged, without a doubt, that God was present in my life. I was sober and had a desire to stay sober. My life was improving in several ways. I had access to a mighty power that was by my side at all times; it never forced itself upon me. The game changing idea about God came to me when I heard in a meeting that I'm no longer responsible for the outcome. I'm only responsible for my effort. It was a liberating concept. God could always teach me a valuable lesson, irrespective of whether I won, lost, or was in a cease-fire in any battle or conflict I was engaged in.

STEP FOUR
GATHERING INTELLIGENCE

*Made a searching and fearless
moral inventory of ourselves.*

Step four is when we compile all the critical information about ourselves. Intelligence is an important aspect of war that's vital to the success of any campaign. Step four is when we make a searching and fearless moral inventory of ourselves. We have to identify what the driving forces of our lives are. Why do we do the things we do? It is a difficult step to implement. We sometimes don't want to look deep within ourselves because we're afraid of what we may find.

I thought the fourth step was completely unnecessary. I believed that I was a pretty nice person most of the time. So why did I have to take an inventory of myself? I thought that if I just removed alcohol from my life, everything would eventually work itself out.

I did agonize for a long time over why I became an alcoholic. Did I drink because of my problems, or were there problems in my life because I drank? I struggled with these questions for a while, constantly going back and forth. The quality of my sobriety wasn't improving much in my battle with alcoholism. I was staying sober physically, but I wasn't getting better emotionally and spiritually. The battle for my heart and soul was still lost.

I finally decided to stop debating the issue and start with the fact that I'm an alcoholic. The origin of my addiction was no longer an issue. I stopped beating myself up for having a disease. I started extending the same compassion to myself that was given to other people who had different diseases and afflictions.

For example, society generally doesn't look down on people who have the dreaded disease of cancer. People don't scold individuals with a bad heart condition. Patients in hospitals with chronic illnesses are usually treated with kindness and sympathy.

Alcoholism and other forms of addiction are often not afforded the same level of compassion. A lot of people incorrectly think that individuals that suffer from addiction "do it to themselves". Sadly, nothing could be further from the truth. I never chose to become an alcoholic. I'm not responsible for my disease. However, I am responsible for my recovery and have to take charge of the situation.

I was told to "keep it simple" many times in the Marine Corps. I apply the wisdom of that saying to the fourth step. I decided I wasn't going to complicate my inventory any more than was necessary. I'm amazed at how difficult some people in recovery make this step. Columns upon columns and pages upon pages with no end in sight! In my experience, the simplest explanation is usually the best.

My method was going to be easy and to the point. What motivated me to do the things I did while I was drinking? The answer was simple: fear. More specifically, it was self-centered fear that manifested itself in various forms. I often acted out in fear because I incorrectly believed that I wasn't good enough or would ever be good enough for anything. I was relieved when I learned that what I did was not as important as why I did it.

The most frightening discovery I made in the fourth step was that most of my fears only

Jonathan D.

existed in my mind and had no basis in reality. It was humbling to admit that my troubles were largely of my own making. Half of the things I worry about have never come true, and the half that does come true usually doesn't turn out to be as bad as I imagined it would.

The wisdom and lessons I learned in the United States Marine Corps continue to help me throughout life. My drill instructors told me often that the greatest enemy I would ever face is the one that exists in my own mind. I can be my own worst enemy. I have sabotaged my own happiness and success more than once. I'm the one who downplays or minimizes anything significant I accomplish. I discovered in step four that I often treat myself terribly. Step four helps me hold myself accountable and stop blaming others.

Another discovery I made in the fourth step is that I have a soul sickness. I have a God-sized hole in my soul that I've tried to fill with everything but God. It took me a long time to acknowledge and admit the emptiness inside me. I thought if I just removed alcohol from my life, everything would turn out fine.

The true nature of my disease began to manifest itself in other ways. I wasn't drinking, but my addictive mind began doing other things excessively. Food, sex, spending money, and working out at the gym are just some of the methods I've used to try and fill up the empty space inside me.

Jonathan D.

Twice a year I go to the VA clinic to get my check-up. My physician always advises me that it would be in my best interest to lose some weight. He doesn't seem to buy the excuse that I "carry it well" because I'm tall. Being a little overweight is a direct result of eating too much in an attempt to alleviate my pain.

Engaging in casual sex was also an unfulfilling and dangerous way to fill the emptiness inside. I used women for selfish pleasure for years because I was trying to run away from the pain inside. I know now that God's daughters should always be treated with dignity and respect and never as mere objects.

Spending money I couldn't afford was another way I tried to treat my sickness. The phrase "spend like a drunken sailor" was definitely true in my case. I have multiple piles of books in my apartment that haven't been read. The books sat untouched for so long that little spiders started building small condos between them!

No matter what I tried, nothing seemed to fix my problem. The only answer to my dilemma was to let my higher power fill me with his influence and love. Nothing in this world has satisfied me like the care and affection that has been given to me by God as I understand him. The only way to get rid of fear and emptiness is to take decisive action. I seek help from my brothers and sisters in the next phase of recovery.

STEP FIVE
BAND OF BROTHERS AND SISTERS

Admitted to God, to ourselves, and to another human being the exact nature of our wrongs.

Step five is another step I had a difficult time with. It took me a while to finally admit my wrongs to myself, God, and another person. Step five seemed difficult to me because I didn't trust anyone. This became more evident after making the transition back to civilian life.

Jonathan D.

I felt like the world was against me; I've been betrayed by so-called friends, and members of my own family have let me down. I didn't receive support when I required it the most.

People hurt me at times with sensitive information that I had shared with them in private. As a result, I was concerned about revealing my deep, dark secrets to anyone. I was not going to allow myself to be hurt again. So, I kept my problems to myself and suffered in silence.

The alienation and isolation individuals can feel from society at times is very contrary to military culture. Veterans and service members are trained to be a part of a team. They live, eat, work, and sleep around each other on a regular basis. We are one team, and we will live and die as one team.

One terrible characteristic of addiction is that it renders its victim extremely lonely. I drank all by myself most of the time and had very few friends. I certainly never felt like a part of any group or team. Complete isolation is one of the outcomes of the disease of addiction. My alcoholism wants me separated and disconnected from people and God so it can slowly and methodically kill me.

My thinking became so distorted that my solution to the problem became worse than the problem. Isolation from everyone is not a good idea when you're dying of loneliness. My solution did not work. I needed to be around other people.

I cannot see myself as I truly am at times. The disease causes me to have an extremely sick and distorted perception of myself. Sharing our thoughts with another human being allows us to examine them from a different and healthier perspective. I can't see the back of my head with my own eyes, but someone else (particularly a sponsor) can. A sponsor is someone we trust to guide us through the steps. We're only as sick as our secrets. I've heard it shared at tables many times that a problem shared is a problem cut in half. A sponsor can hold me accountable and not co-sign any of my bullshit.

Men and women in the service are accustomed

to holding each other accountable. I was taught that there are certain principles and standards that every Marine should follow. Not living up to these standards and principles resulted in being disciplined by superiors. Showing up to formation or work late wasn't tolerated. Not having your room or uniform squared away was pointed out without mercy. The men and women of the Armed Forces are a band of brothers and sisters who push each other to achieve excellence.

Alcoholics and addicts tend to be extremely defiant people by nature. We don't take kindly to someone waving their finger and telling us what to do. In certain relationships, the addict is usually treated as inferior. The family thinks

Jonathan D.

he isn't cooperating, his doctor thinks he's hopeless, and employers see him as someone unreliable for anything important. For a long time, even the courts viewed the alcoholic as a dangerous criminal that needed to be locked up or put in a mental facility. Some churches unfortunately take the position that the alcoholic or addict is nothing more than a degenerate sinner. It's refreshing to have someone listen you with a sympathetic ear and still hold you to a high standard.

Step five really is the step that can make us feel closest to God as we understand him because it assures us that we're not alone in a world that can be hostile and violent. We are finally able to relinquish all our wrongs to a power of our own understanding and start to feel forgiven. We begin to feel good because we realize we're worthy of forgiveness.

Many veterans have secrets they're reluctant to share with God or another human being. Many vets who have served in the combat zone have seen, committed, or experienced incidents that can only be described as horrific. They have seen human cruelty and carnage at its absolute worse. The pain and suffering they witness can cause psychological wounds that take years to heal. Sometimes, the pain of addiction becomes too great and an alarming number of veterans take their own lives.

Step five is a wonderful opportunity for veterans to share their pain with a higher power and another human being who is sympathetic to what they've been through. It's extremely therapeutic to share sensitive details with someone and know you won't be judged, ridiculed, or betrayed. All that's required is the willingness to humble ourselves before God and each other.

I often find it ironic that the step I avoided the most turned out to be the one I needed the most. We don't have to carry around all that guilt and pain anymore. We can become free to move on with our lives and become the men and women we were intended to be.

STEP SIX

THE NEXT EVOLUTION

Were entirely ready to have God remove all these defects of character.

Step six is when we to take our program of recovery to the next level. It's when we begin to reach farther in our quest to find new freedom. It's the step wherein we want to be free of the defects of character that prevent us from being useful to our fellow human beings.

Jonathan D.

Being entirely ready to have God remove these defects of character was just as difficult as admitting defeat for me. It was hard for me to accept the fact that I couldn't fix myself no matter how hard I tried. My experience in the Marine Corps, combined with my upbringing, taught me that I could accomplish anything I set my mind to. All I had to do is apply enough willpower and intelligence and I would achieve any goal. It's not surprising that the remnants of my past come back to haunt me. It's as though I only want to give God the addiction problem and take care of the rest myself.

I define a defect of character as anything that stands in the way of me being useful to another person. Anything that stops me from providing maximum service to my brothers and sisters must be removed by my higher power. I have to be willing to let God use me in any way he sees fit. Only he has the power to remove obstacles and roadblocks that hinder my effectiveness.

One thing we have to keep in mind about step six is that we're not adding anything to ourselves. Instead, we're having our harmful thoughts and tendencies removed from our thinking and behavior. Our selfishness and self-centeredness has to be removed in order for our compassion to reveal itself in vivid detail

Defects that are out of our control can prevent us from growing and feeling better about ourselves. I no longer want to feel excessive amounts of envy, greed, anger, and frustration.

Jonathan D.

I have to be willing to let God mold me into a useful person; I desperately need to heal instead of being sick and tired all the time.

My approach to step six was completely wrong in my first years of recovery. It was difficult for me to admit and accept that I was a broken person who required help. I used to tell one of my sponsors how I'll fix this and I'll fix that about myself. My sponsor informed me that the process doesn't work that way. God as we understand him makes the changes happen. I have to allow God to do for me what I can't do for myself once again. If I had the power to fix myself, I would have done it a long time ago.

We don't have to be perfect in order to be effective. God as I understand him likes to use broken people on occasion to do his work. The reason I think God is fond of using broken people like us is because he wants to get full credit for our success. God's power is demonstrated in all its glory when broken people become willing to tap into it.

The military requires high standards in terms of behavior and character. My officers and non-commissioned officers always encouraged me to set the bar really high. Values like commitment, honor, courage, and dedication come back into our lives with full force once our defects are removed.

The United States military is without equal. We are indeed a special force for good in the world. We, as recovering veterans and service members,

Jonathan D.

can feel proud that we are being helped and being used by God as we understand him to showcase his massive strength in the greatest fighting force on the planet.

STEP SEVEN
WEAKNESS LEAVING THE BODY

*Humbly asked Him to remove
our shortcomings.*

The first word in step seven is another word some veterans aren't comfortable with. Step seven instructs us to humbly ask God as we understand him to remove our shortcomings. It can be difficult at times for veterans and service members to be humble when they're constantly reminded they're the best of the best. I thought humility was a form of weakness. I was convinced I would be taken advantage of if I was too nice or humble.

It wasn't until recovery that I learned the true meaning of the word humility. Being humble simply means I can be taught something new and significant. If I remain cocky and arrogant for too long, I'll never learn anything new and will be stuck on stupid for several years to come.

I like to follow the lead of my sponsor who has over thirty years of sobriety under his belt. He says that he'll have to keep coming back to meetings because he doesn't have everything figured out yet. He's humble enough to know that he still has much to learn about sobriety and recovery even though he hasn't had a drink in decades. The ability to be humble is actually a sign of intelligence. The ones who perish from the disease of addiction are the ones who, for whatever reason, can't learn from their mistakes.

We don't always have to be humiliated to learn humility, even though a lot of us learned lessons the hard way. We had to be beaten down to the point where we were willing to listen to reason. We had to be brought to our knees before God because there wasn't anyone else to turn to. We had to be the ones whose hands got burned fifty times on the hot stove before discovering that putting them there wasn't a good idea.

Jonathan D.

I remember my platoon in boot camp being punished with extra physical training every time we made a mistake. I don't think we won a single event in boot camp, but we certainly became strong guys when it was over. Pain does have some benefits. It brought me to Alcoholics Anonymous and gave me a relationship with God as I understand him. However, I no longer see the point in making the same mistakes over and over. I'm at a point in my life and recovery where I want to learn from other people's mistakes.

Overcoming weakness was drilled into my head during boot camp. I've also learned techniques such as behavior modification, positive thinking, and visualization. These practices are excellent methods that a person can use to improve their life. A person should think positively and visualize a successful outcome. A person should modify their behavior and "act their way" into a new thought process.

However, these methods alone haven't eliminated the shortcomings in my life that have afflicted me and interfered with my usefulness to other people. I would still have thoughts that I didn't want to no matter how much I tried to think positively. I would still act out in inappropriate ways after repeated attempts at behavior modification. These shortcomings never seemed to go away because I wasn't doing what the step instructed me to do.

It was only when I humbled myself before God

Jonathan D.

as I understand him that changes of any real consequence took place. God's power changed me in a way nothing else could. The destructive and hurtful shortcomings that torture me and cause turmoil dissipate over time in a way that can only be described as miraculous. The process is similar to the experience of weakness leaving the body that I had in boot camp. The true nature of my character started coming to light as a result of this cleansing process.

STEP EIGHT
DAMAGE CONTROL

Made a list of all persons we had harmed, and became willing to make amends to them all.

Alcoholics and addicts cause massive amounts of death and destruction not only their lives, but also in the lives of others. Our loved ones suffer tremendously while we're in the grips of our addiction. We break promises and never seem to be around when we're needed. The emotional, psychological, and physical wounds we inflict can take many years to heal.

Just like in war, a pile of debris and bodies have to be cleaned up after the fighting has stopped. Step eight is when we look at the damage we have caused and formulate a plan to amend and rectify the harm we are responsible for. It can be a gruesome and horrifying experience to confront the people whose lives we made a living hell. A lot of courage is required to confront people who in some cases never wanted to see us again.

It must be remembered that we were extremely sick people when all the havoc was caused. Our bodies and minds were poisoned to the point where we couldn't tell the difference between kindness and cruelty. However, we still have to answer for the devastation we created without any reservations.

I used several excuses to avoid step eight in the early stages of my recovery. The disease itself was used as an excuse. Why should an alcoholic or addict have to make amends for acting inappropriately during his addiction? We are reminded in meetings that the addict has lost the power of choice and his willpower is useless. Yet, all of a sudden, he is supposed to be responsible for all his actions when he gets to step eight. There appears to be an inconsistency here as well as a double standard. The alcoholic is being treated harsher than people with other illnesses.

Jonathan D.

Another obstacle that prevented me from implementing step eight was having a victim mindset. For years on end, I believed I never did anything wrong. I was the one born into a violent alcoholic home. I was the one raised by a step-father who routinely beat me and told me what I couldn't do or become; I was the one who was often neglected by a mother who suffered from mental illness. As far as I was concerned, the world owed me amends.

The truth is that I looked at the world the way I looked at myself and didn't see it the way it really was. I hated my fellow man because I didn't like the person staring back at me in the mirror. I treated and viewed people harshly because deep down I felt as though I would never measure up to my ridiculous standards.

I expected too much of myself and everyone around me. The Marine Corps taught me to have high standards, but mine were simply unachievable. I considered myself a worthless failure if I made even one mistake. I was ready to kill someone for accidently bumping into me. My harsh treatment of people was due to a fragile and hypersensitive nature that was easily agitated. The attitude and actions of everyone around me were interpreted as a threat to my existence. I defended myself all the time like it was fourth and goal with only two seconds left in the game.

Veterans and service members are taught to be

accountable for their actions. Can we honestly use some of these reasons as an excuse to not make amends? We can't use the disease as an excuse because we weren't under the influence every time we hurt someone. We often hurt people in various ways simply because we wanted to. We took our pain and frustrations out on people who didn't cause the problem and had nothing to do with it.

The fire inside of us was burning long before we picked up a drink or drug. Alcohol was the fuel that made the spark turn into an inferno. It's our responsibility to clean up the ashes and bring about restitution to others as a part of our recovery. We have to answer for all the wrongs we did to other people. Everyone has to be put on the list. There are some people we won't be able to make our amends to, but at least we're willing to try.

It's important for me to put myself on the list as well. I've hurt myself just as bad or worse as I've hurt others. The way I've treated myself is absolutely terrible. If I treated others the way I've treated myself sometimes, I would probably be in prison right now. The man in the mirror, staring back at me, deserves to be treated better than the way I've treated him. He deserves amends as much as anyone.

STEP NINE

RESPONSIBILITY FOR OUR ACTIONS

Made direct amends to such people wherever possible, except when to do so would injure them or others.

It's a truly liberating experience to visit people we wounded and take responsibility for our actions by making amends to them. I love watching the psychological and emotional injuries I have inflicted get restored and repaired. A tremendous amount of courage is required to make amends to those we have harmed.

Bravery is a trait that veterans and service members have in spades. They face their fears and rush into battle to confront whatever dangers await them. Courage is a state of mind that has to be cultivated and practiced on a regular basis. All the training and experience veterans have received comes in handy when we make the decision to right the wrongs we have committed.

There's no way to know how the other person is going to react. It's uncertain if the affected person is going to give us a warm reception and gratefully accept our heartfelt attempt to amend our past behavior, or reply in a hostile and violent manner. We have no control over how others are going to respond. People have a right to think and feel the way they want to. Some people choose to hold on to anger, grudges, and resentments for years and refuse to let go. There's always a risk when making amends, but it's a risk worth taking.

We have to remember that amends should never be made if they're going to cause damage to ourselves or others. Some information just shouldn't be shared because it can cause massive amounts of emotional, spiritual, and psychological pain. Our recovery and life could be set back tremendously as a result, which would neutralize our usefulness to others.

Jonathan D.

Some veterans returning home from wars, like those in Iraq and Afghanistan, committed acts in war that they may feel the need to make amends for. It's up to each person to decide whether or not that's an appropriate course of action. The line between "following orders" and acting as a rational individual with autonomy isn't always clear. Some veterans can move on with their lives with little difficulty, while others carry around a lot of guilt.

Some wrongs may never be righted, but the attempt must be made if the opportunity presents itself. Step nine is a step where we're showing the world through our actions that God as we understand him is changing us, that we're moving closer and closer toward a spiritual awakening. Words alone aren't going to do the job. Actions speak louder than a fancy speech. People get really tired of hearing alcoholics and addicts say "I'm sorry", or "I'll never do that again" only to be hurt time after time.

The best way to make amends is to stay clean and sober. One, five, or ten years of sobriety and clean time has the tendency to raise eyebrows and grab people's attention. On the other hand, if a person starts drinking or using again, then all bets are off. All the so-called apologies in the world will enter in one ear and exit out the other. At that point, people couldn't care less what you have to say.

The healing that takes place during process of making amends is incredible. My life started to change in miraculous ways. I no longer felt like a worthless failure that didn't have anything to offer to anyone. My past doesn't hold me hostage anymore and is now being used for something useful. I don't feel self-pity like I used to. I now know that I'm not alone and that there are numerous people struggling with the same issues I am.

Changes and promises will materialize in my life only if I take action. I can't sit around and "hope" they become reality. The Marine Corps taught me that positive thinking has to be combined with positive action in order to get results. The military and twelve-step recovery are both action oriented. The old-timers told me to get off my ass and do something! My life and recovery were not going to improve by sitting around and doing nothing. I had to put into practice what I've learned.

We tried to think ourselves into a new way of thinking and couldn't do it. We tried to think ourselves into a new way of acting and couldn't do it. The only success I've had is when I acted my way into a new way of thinking. Veterans and service members are used to grinding it out in order to move forward with the mission.

STEP TEN
ASSESSMENT OF THE SITUATION

*Continued to take personal inventory and when
we were wrong promptly admitted it.*

Step ten is when we seek better ways to improve our lives and program by continuing to take personal inventory and admitting when we're wrong. The greatest lesson I learned in the Marine Corps is how to improvise, adapt, and overcome any challenge in life. Life is a war that

Jonathan D.

changes on a daily basis. We constantly face new challenges that threaten our well-being and happiness. Unfamiliar threats require unique and innovative strategies. Step ten is the step where we assess the situation of our recovery.

A spot-check inventory is crucial to identify the thinking patterns that can get out of hand at a moment's notice. Problems we couldn't care less about yesterday suddenly become catastrophic today. Attitudes, strategies, and tactics have to be flexible because what may have worked weeks or even days ago has to be modified now in order to respond to new expectations and demands.

Our thinking has to be constantly monitored in order to ensure that self-defeating and self-destructive ideas are dealt with swiftly and efficiently, otherwise, harmful ideas can escalate exponentially. We have to be on guard against the emotions and thoughts that can ruin a good day.

The military trains its members to be ready to defend this country at a moment's notice. Our senses and adrenalin levels are usually in a heightened state. We're ready for battle at all times. It can be stressful and difficult to defuse aggressive tendencies that are out of our control.

I've been sober for years and can still fly off the deep end into a fit of rage and frustration due to a lack of patience. Anger and resentment can rise in me to the point where I think I'm

Jonathan D.

going to explode. I feel my blood boil and go into attack mode. It's then that I have to take several deep breaths and ask God as I understand him for help. The military taught me to remain calm under pressure. I now use these waiting times as great opportunities to practice breath control, meditation, and prayer.

I have to ask for help whenever harmful thoughts creep into my mind. I don't have the power to get rid of my destructive thinking and emotions. Only the strength of a higher power can soothe me and calm me down. Only God can stop the war I have with myself and everyone around me. I only feel protected from the hostile voices within when God puts me in his safe zone.

I remind myself all the time that I'm never going

to be completely cured of alcoholism. I'm never going to wake up one fine day and have the disease completely removed. The good news is that God as we understand him can give us a daily stay of execution if we maintain a close spiritual connection with him. So I concentrate my efforts on taking one day at a time.

It's important to focus only on one day at a time because it takes a larger goal and breaks it down into something more manageable. My drill instructors in boot camp always told us to concentrate our efforts on the task at hand instead of the grueling thirteen weeks ahead. Don't even think about not using or drinking for the rest of your life. Focus only on today. The goal may be permanent abstinence, but only think about the next twenty-four hours and, before you know it, the days will turn into months and years.

Promptly admitting when we're wrong is crucial because we have to correct our mistakes and learn from them. There's nothing wrong with making mistakes. I've learned more from failure than I've ever learned from success. The problem arises when I don't learn from my mistakes and keep repeating them. Step ten tells me that when I'm wrong or have made a mistake, I have to promptly own up to it.

Step ten encourages us to constantly evaluate our bad judgement and behavior just like in the military. What could we have done better? What is the proper way to do what we did wrong? How can we learn from others who have what we want? I have come to accept that I don't know everything or have all the answers.

It's a hard fact of life that there are people in this world who are smarter, more efficient, and more productive than me. I don't resent these people like I used to. I actively seek out their wise advice and counsel because I've found that they're usually more than willing to help me if I ask them to. As a result, I can learn from them and move on to the next phase of my recovery and life.

STEP ELEVEN
MARCHING ORDERS

Sought through prayer and meditation to improve our conscious contact with God <u>as we understood Him</u>, praying only for knowledge of His will for us and the power to carry that out.

Step eleven is when we get to have our personal time with God and receive our marching orders. We ask God for guidance through prayer and meditation. I think of God as my commander in chief. He has an open-door policy that allows me to approach him anytime I need to.

God as I understand him makes me aware of my mission and what's expected of me. He lays out his position regarding why he's kept me around all this time. He explains the reasons why I'm not dead or in prison (even though he could still use me if I was incarcerated).

I have a degree in Philosophy, so I seek to know the deeper reasons for why I went through what I did. God explains his answer in a way that my military mind can understand: My mission is to help alcoholics and addicts struggling with addiction. The process I went through is similar to that of making a weapon.

Swords go through several stages when they're being manufactured. They start out as a piece of metal that's constantly beaten, pounded, and grinded. They then go through intense heat and fire in order to get purified. Finally, they get sharpened and polished until they become magnificent weapons of war. God as we understand him was forging us into powerful instruments to be used in the battle against addiction.

I like that the word "power" is mentioned in the eleventh step because it's a neat reminder of what my real problem still is. I need God's power in my life at all times. The ability to fight wars has to be backed by overwhelming force.

Jonathan D.

It's good to know we don't have to go into battle empty-handed.

Step eleven instructs me to pray in a manner that differs from the way I used to communicate with my higher power. I ask God in prayer to watch over my friends and family. I pray he gets or keeps my fellow alcoholics and addicts clean and sober. I pray that the friends and family members of addicts be healed from the devastating effects of living with addiction. The service men and women in harm's way are also included in my prayers. I pray that they return home to their families safely.

I ask God what I can do for him instead of what he can do for me. I ask for guidance and strength to carry out his will for me and the people I care about. I was told early in recovery to ask God for help in the morning and give thanks at night. God's will is so great that I now give thanks in advance for the imminent success and victory in the morning and give praise at night. We win the fight first and then go into battle. We never go into battle first and then hope to win.

The practice of meditation is instrumental to having serenity and peace of mind. It can be difficult for us to relax and shut off all the noise that is in our minds. Veterans and service members are in attack mode for a good majority of the time, and high levels of stress and aggression are common. One reason I drank was to silence the thoughts that were out of control.

It took me a lot of practice to sit still for just five minutes and breathe deeply. I've gradually increased this duration, and the results have been incredible. The answers I seek always come to me when I'm calm, peaceful, and open to instruction. My cares and worries are removed and I can go about my day.

Step eleven comprises final stages and rounds to prepare us to go out and carry the message to other alcoholics and addicts. The process reminds me of the final phase of Marine boot camp when the battalion commander inspects every Marine to determine whether he graduates. Likewise, God as we understand him gives us a final look-over before he sends us out into the field.

Everything must be in proper order because we have important work to do. Our spiritual, emotional, and physical condition must be in good shape. We have to set a good example because we can't preach what we don't practice.

The anticipation starts to build and we can barely contain our excitement. We're eager to pass along what was freely given to us. We're like lions getting ready to go on a hunt and look for fresh meat. God gives us his final remarks and then sounds the bell, letting us out of the gate. We then rush out into the world with the force of a tsunami.

STEP TWELVE
NO ONE LEFT BEHIND

Having had a spiritual awakening as a result of these steps, we tried to carry this message to alcoholics, and to practice these principles in all our affairs .

The day I became a United States Marine was one of the proudest of my life. I completed the training only a handful of people can and became a member of one of the finest military organizations in the world. I was ready to kill

Jonathan D.

America's enemies when called upon to do so. I had a similar feeling when I experienced a spiritual awakening as a result of working the twelve steps. God became an experienced reality in my life instead of some abstract idea that I had read about in a philosophy book or the Bible. I felt as though I had been shaped and molded to go to war against the disease of addiction.

The transformation that takes place in step twelve is a sight to see. Watching people recover from a hopeless state of mind, body, and soul has constituted the most enjoyable moments of my life. My dream is to watch every addict experience a new freedom from the disease of addiction. Step twelve is when we go out into the world and bring our brothers and sisters home. We don't want anyone left behind.

The twelfth step allows us to carry this message to other alcoholics and addicts and strike back at the disease that pounded us senseless for years. Our addictions tortured us physically, mentally, spiritually, and psychologically for years. We woke up every morning terrified of what we did or said the night before. Our minds and life were filled with unbearable amounts of guilt and shame. The twelfth step provides us with a great opportunity for some payback.

Carrying the message to other addicts and helping them get or stay clean and sober is our way of getting back at the disease, the battle being won every time a drunk puts down a drink or an addict doesn't use. Whenever we help someone, the grip addiction has over them becomes weaker and weaker. We all can look the disease straight in the eye and say "You're not going to kill me or anyone I care about today".

We "try" to carry the message to others who still suffer. Plans in life and war don't always go as expected. The disease of addiction is a formidable foe that shouldn't be underestimated even for a second. There are going to be casualties in this conflict because some people won't be ready to accept help for whatever reason. However, if we can help one alcoholic or addict stay clean and sober for one day, all our efforts were not in vain. If we gain only an inch of territory every few days we're still making progress.

The process of recovery is absolutely fascinating. I've watched people arrive in terrible condition, just like I once was. They were physically, mentally, and spiritually devastated. A large number were suicidal. Within weeks these same people were seen laughing, smiling, and joking. They made coffee, gave other members rides to meetings, and chaired meetings themselves. It's hard to believe that they were the same people who came in just a short time ago.

Incredible things happen when addicts get together as a team and help each other. I'm blessed to be a part of such an incredible formula for recovery. I tell people I believe in miracles

Jonathan D.

because I am one and witness them on a regular basis. I've watched a power greater than me transform human wreckage into something useful. Carrying the message to addicts and alcoholics gives them another chance to live healthy and productive lives which benefits our Armed Forces and society as a whole.

The military emphasizes values such as honor, integrity, courage, and commitment. The twelve steps reestablished a code in my life for proper and healthy living. The steps gave me back what the military instilled in me. Today, I treat people with respect because that's the way I want to be treated. I take pride in my appearance and how I present myself to the world. The line between right and wrong is now clear and distinct. I once again have order and discipline that allows me to live with high standards.

The fight against addiction is not easy. Recovery is hard work. Some days will be tougher than others, but we will stay in the fight and grind it out until our dying breath. We will not stop until as many addicts as possible are helped. We will be a constant thorn in the side of addiction. We will never fight fair and will use every trick in the book to help someone stay clean and sober. The new freedom we experience will be sweet and satisfying.

THE TWELVE STEPS OF ALCOHOLICS ANONYMOUS*

1. We admitted we were powerless over alcohol-that our lives had become unmanageable.

2. Came to believe that a Power greater than ourselves could restore us to sanity.

3. Made a decision to turn our will and our lives over to the care of God *as we understood Him.*

4. Made a searching and fearless moral inventory of ourselves.

5. Admitted to God, to ourselves, and to another human being the exact nature of our wrongs.

6. Were entirely ready to have God remove all these defects of character.

7. Humbly asked Him to remove our shortcomings.

8. Made a list of all persons we had harmed, and became willing to make amends to them all.

9. Made direct amends to such people wherever possible, except when to do so would injure them or others.

10. Continued to take personal inventory and when we were wrong promptly admitted it.

11. Sought through prayer and meditation to improve our conscious contact with God *as we understood Him*, praying only for knowledge of His will for us and the power to carry that out.

12. Having had a spiritual awakening as the result of these steps, we tried to carry this message to alcoholics, and to practice these principles in all our affairs.

*The Twelve Steps are reprinted with permission of Alcoholics Anonymous World Services, Inc. ("A.A.W.S."). Permission to reprint the Twelve

Jonathan D.

Steps does not mean that A.A.W.S. has reviewed or approved the contents of the publication, or that A.A. necessarily agrees with the views expressed herein. A.A. is a program of recovery from alcoholism only-use of the Twelve Steps in connection with programs and activities which are patterned after A.A., but which address other problems, or in any other non-A.A., does not imply otherwise.

Printed in the USA
CPSIA information can be obtained
at www.ICGtesting.com
LVHW090521280824
789504LV00003B/313